القواعد الفقهية

MAXIMS OF FIQH

(AL-QAWĀ'ID AL-FIQHIYYAH)

BY SHAYKH
'ABDUR-RAHMĀN BIN NĀSIR AS-SA'DĪ
رحمه الله

Translated by Abū Fātimah Azhar Majothi

دار مكة العالمية للنشر والتوزيع
DAR MAKKAH
INTERNATIONAL
PUBLISHING AND DISTRIBUTION

First Edition 1436 AH / 2015 CE

ISBN 978-1-911448-96-9 ردمك

Printed and Distributed by:

Dar Makkah International
23-25 Parliament Street
Birmingham UK
B10 0QJ
Tel: 00 217739309
0021 7723 600
Mob: 00 447533177 345
0044 7815806 517

دار مكة المكرمة
42 ش البستان متفرع من ش الجلاء
المنصورة
مصر
0502345627
0195520475

Translation and typesetting by:
Abū Fātimah Azhar Majothī
www.ihsaandesign.com

Translation based on the text verified by Dr Sulayman bin ʿAbdullah Aba al-Khayl, second edition 1430/2009

الْقَوَاعِدُ الْفِقْهِيَّةُ

بسم الله الرحمن الرحيم

CONTENTS

A SHORT BIOGRAPHY OF SHAYKH AL-SA'DI

He is the *'Allāmah,* the *Faqīh,* the *Usūlī,* the *Zāhid* and *Shaykh* of al-Qasīm: Abū 'Abdullāh 'Abdur-Rahmān bin Nāsir bin 'Abdullāh bin Nāsir bin Hamd, from the family of Sa'dī, at-Tamīmī (which is from the tribe of Banū Tamīm). He was born in Unayzah, located in the province of al-Qasīm, Saudi Arabia, on the 12th of Muharram, in the year 1307 A.H.

By the age of eight years, the Shaykh lost both his mother and father. Before his death, the Shaykh's father took great care of his children's upbringing and entrusted his eldest son Hamd with nurturing them. Consequently, Hamd made great efforts in providing the Shaykh with a righteous environment and encouraged him to seek knowledge. The Shaykh began his studies by completing his memorisation of the Qur'ān, which he finished by the age of 11, after which he continued by studying the Islāmic sciences including: Tafsīr, Hadīth and its sciences, 'Aqīdah, Usūl, the Arabic language, etc. and paid great attention to the books of Shaykh-ul-Islām Ibnu Taymiyyah, and his student Shaykh-ul-Islām Ibnu Qayyim.

The Shaykh began teaching at the age of 23 years and combined both learning and teaching by spending his time reading to his teachers or teaching his pupils or revising and researching his books; he continued upon this methodology until he became an Imām amongst the people of knowledge.

The Shaykh studied the Islāmic sciences at the feet of several scholars, from them:

1. Shaykh Ibrāhīm bin Hamd bin Jāsir (d.1337 A.H.);
2. Shaykh Sālih bin 'Uthmān al-Qādī (d.1351 A.H.);
3. Shaykh Muhammad al-Amīn ash-Shinqītī (d.1351 A.H.).

The Shaykh taught many students, the most senior of those being:

1. Shaykh 'Abdullah bin 'Abdul-'Azīz bin 'Aqīl ﷬
2. Shaykh Muhammad bin Sālih al-'Uthaymīn ﷬
3. Shaykh 'Abdullāh bin 'Abdur-Rahmān al-Bassām ﷬
4. Shaykh 'Abdul-'Azīz bin Muhammad as-Salmān

The Shaykh authored many works, some of which have been published while others are still in manuscript form. From the most famous published works are:

1. *Taysīr-ul-Karīmir-Rahmān fī Tafsīr Kalāmil-Mannān*;
2. *Manhaj-us-Sālikīn wa Tawdīh-ul-Fiqh fid-Dīn*,;
3. *Al-Qawl-us-Sadīd fī Maqāsid-it-Tawhīd*;
4. *Jawāmi'-ul-Akhbār* and its explanation entitled *Bahjatu Qulūbil Abrār wa Qurrut 'Uyūnil-Akhyār fī Sharh Jawāmi'-ul-Akhbār.*

The Shaykh died on Thursday, the 23nd of Jamād-ul-Ākhirah, 1376 A.H. (corresponding to 1957 C.E.) after patiently suffering several illnesses for five years prior to his demise. May Allāh have mercy on us and the Shaykh and gather us and him with the righteous in al-Jannah. Āmīn!

Translator's Note

The maxims of *fiqh*, or *al-qawā'id al-fiqhiyyah*, are part of a specific science which falls under the category of *fiqh*. A maxim is defined as a general rule by which subsidiary *fiqh* rulings are known by directly.[1]

The maxims of *fiqh* are mostly comprehensive statements which combine multiple subsidiary issues which resemble one another in purpose and deduction, while others are based on specific Quranic verses[2] or Hadith[3].

There are five maxims which are considered all-encompassing, and many *fuqahā* refer issues of *fiqh* to them; they are commonly referred to as the all-encompassing great maxims of fiqh, or *al-qawā'id al-fiqhiyyah al-kulliyyah al-kubrā*; they are:

1. All matters are considered by their intentions.	١. الأمور بمقاصدها.
2. Certainty is not removed by doubt.	٢. اليقين لا يزال بالشك.
3. Hardship entails ease.	٣. المشقة تجلب التيسير.

[1] حكم أغلبي يتعرف منه أحكام الجزئيات الفقهية المباشرة. See *al-Qawā'id al-Fiqhiyyah* page 50 onwards.

[2] Such as maxim four in this book.

[3] Such as maxim one in this book.

4. Harm is to be eliminated. ٤. الضرر يزال.

5. Customary practises are legislative. ٥. العادة محكمة.

The first book to be dedicated to this science was penned by Imām al-Karkhī al-Hanafī (d. 340 AH) and is known as *Usūl al-Karkhī*; it contains 39 principles, some of which are considered maxims while others are *dawābit* (precepts). Over the centuries, scholars from the different *madhhabs* have contributed to the science and the author of this work, Imām al-Sa'dī ﷺ has no less than three books on the subject alone.

For more information and details about the maxims of *fiqh,* the reader may refer to the highly beneficial introduction by Dr. Muhammad b. 'Abd al-Ghaffār al-Sharīf to the book on maxims, *al-Majmū' al-Mudhhab fī Qawā'id al-Madhhab* by Imam al-'Alā'ī al-Shāfi (d. 761 AH).[4]

---

[4] Printed by the Ministry of Endowments and Islamic Affairs, published in 1414 AH / 1994 CE.

القواعد الفقهية

[The Reason Why The Shaykh Wrote This Book]

All praise belongs to Allah who enlightened His slaves with the principles of rulings, and elucidated and unravelled to them what is lawful and what is not; He further facilitated for them knowledge and action through the religion of Islam.

I praise Him for His immense favours and I thank Him for His tremendous graces; I seek forgiveness from Him and repent to Him from all sins and vices; I further ask Him for aid and direction in all that I intend and wish to accomplish, for no matter or goal can be completed except with the help of the All-Knowing King; I supplicate (to Allah) for peace and blessings to be bestowed on Muhammad, the master of mankind, and a shining lamp in the darkness, and (I ask for the same to be bestowed) on his family, his companions and their successors throughout the days, and successively over time.

I previously dictated to some students important maxims and comprehensive rules except that they required elucidation, clarification and examples to realise and uncover them; I was asked to add a light commentary to these maxims by which the aforementioned goal may be achieved, so I sought Allah's aid and I commenced this blessed explanation.

I ask Allah, the Generous, to help me in this endeavour and facilitate it for me; and there is no ability or power except by Allah's permission.

[INTRODUCTION]

In the name of Allah, the All-Merciful, the Bestower of Mercy.

All praise belongs to Allah, the Lord of all creation. May Allah send peace and blessings on Muhammad, his family and all his Companions.

What follows are comprehensive fiqh maxims, which apply to multiple issues, which the student of knowledge will find indispensable:

القاعدة الأولى: الأمور بمقاصدها

MAXIM ONE: ALL MATTERS ARE CONSIDERED BY THEIR INTENTIONS

Know, that this maxim, contains tremendous benefit and combines a great deal. Its evidence is the hadīth of 'Umar ﷺ who said: I heard the Messenger of Allah ﷺ say:

« إنما الأعمال بالنيات وإنما لكل امرئ ما نوى »

> "Actions are only by intentions; and every man will only have what he intended.'"

The hadīth is agreed upon (by al-Bukhārī and Muslim).[5]

This maxim applies to all acts of worship, such as ablution, *tayammum*, the ritual bath and the prayer, be it obligatory or supererogatory, an individual duty or a collective one; likewise, zakāt, fasting and *i'tikāf*, be it obligatory or supererogatory; (it also includes) expiations, jihād, the manumission of slaves, conditional manumission (upon the death of the master) and emancipation contracts - meaning by that, one is able to attain reward for these four things depending on whether he intended seek nearness to Allah thereby.

[5] Sahih al-Bukhari (1) and Muslim (1907).

In fact, this is applicable to all permissible actions (*mubāhāt*), when one intends nearness to Allah with a pious intention to obey Him and he prepares himself to actively perform worship, such as eating, drinking, sleeping, earning money, marriage and having marital sexual relations, and even for the woman when she intends chasteness, conceiving a child or increasing the Muslim population in number.

BENEFIT: one of the matters for which a person's intention is not taken to account, and which the *fuqahā* refer to as *turūk*, is whatever one means to remove and free himself from, such as removing an impurity from the body, or clothing or place. The intention is not stipulated in doing such things.[6]

[6] Likewise, staying clear from committing fornication, stealing and all other sins; it is not stipulated that one makes an intention to leave these matters as the requirement of the Sharia is achieved by merely abstaining from them, even if a person does not actively intend to do so. See *al-Majmū'a al-Madhhab* by Imam al-'Alā'ī al-Shāfi'ī (1/256).

القاعدة الثانية – ويدخل تحتها ثلاث قواعد:

أحدها: الضرورات تبيح المحظورات

MAXIM TWO IS COMPRISED OF THREE SUB-MAXIMS[7]:

1. NECESSITIES LEGALISE PROHIBITIONS

Meaning: when a *mukallif* (a sane, mature Muslim who is responsible for carrying out Islamic duties) is compelled to carry out a prohibition because he fears some kind of harm on himself if he does not do so, then such a matter becomes legal (*mubāh*) for him, due to the saying of [Allāh] the Most High:

﴿ وَمَا جَعَلَ عَلَيْكُمْ فِي ٱلدِّينِ مِنْ حَرَجٍ ﴾

> **"And (He) has not laid upon you in religion any hardship..." [22:78]**

And His saying, the Most High:

﴿ يُرِيدُ ٱللَّهُ بِكُمُ ٱلْيُسْرَ وَلَا يُرِيدُ بِكُمُ ٱلْعُسْرَ ﴾

> **"Allah intends for you ease, and He does not want to make things difficult for you." [2:185]**

---

7 The maxim in short, is: "harm is to be eliminated (الضرر يزال)".

And His saying, the Most High:

﴿ فَمَنِ ٱضْطُرَّ غَيْرَ بَاغٍ وَلَا عَادٍ فَلَآ إِثْمَ عَلَيْهِ ۚ إِنَّ ٱللَّهَ غَفُورٌ رَّحِيمٌ ﴾

"[He has forbidden you only dead animals, and blood, and the flesh of swine, and that which is slaughtered as a sacrifice for other than Allâh] but if one is forced by necessity without wilful disobedience or transgressing due limits, then there is no sin on Him." [2:173]

There are innumerable scenarios in which this maxim applies, such as eating carrion, drinking impure water and other things, all of which are permitted in times of necessity. Another example is multiple and consecutive movements in a prayer; this does not nullify the prayer. Likewise, the prohibited matters during *al-ihram*; if the pilgrim is compelled to do a prohibited action then it is permitted, but he is required to offer an expiation (*al-fidyah*). Likewise, the marriage between a free man and a slave girl is not permissible except in the case when committing a sin is feared and self-restraint is unachievable. [Likewise,] whoever is compelled to take the wealth of another, such as in the form of food or otherwise, it is permissible to take it without the permission or agreement of its owner except in the case when it would harm its owner. This is because something harmful cannot be removed by another thing which is harmful. And we find a range of matters which, when one is compelled to do, are legalised.

In relation to this [maxim], there is a statement the *fuqāhā* often repeat: "There is no prohibition in the event of necessity, or obligation in the absence of capability."[8]

[8] لا محرم مع اضطرار ولا واجب مع عدم اقتدار

والثانية: الحاجات تزيل المكروهات

2. NEEDS ELIMINATE DISLIKES

That is, when there is a need to carry out a disliked matter, then its being disliked (*makrūh*) is lifted, and any matter which is disliked to leave, its being disliked is lifted if there is a need to leave it. This is based on the saying of [Allāh] the Most High:

﴿ وَمَا جَعَلَ عَلَيْكُمْ فِي ٱلدِّينِ مِنْ حَرَجٍ ﴾

"And (Allah) has not laid upon you in religion any hardship." [22:78]

[And the saying of the Most High:]

﴿ يُرِيدُ ٱللَّهُ بِكُمُ ٱلْيُسْرَ وَلَا يُرِيدُ بِكُمُ ٱلْعُسْرَ ﴾

"Allah intends for you ease and He does not want to make things difficult for you." [2:185]

And due to the saying of Messenger of Allah ﷺ:

« إن الدين يسر »

"The religion is easy."

This hadīth is agreed on (by al-Bukhārī and Muslim).[9]

There are innumerable scenarios in which this principle applies to, such as: the types of water which are to disliked to use, like water whose state is altered without mixing with other liquids, or used water for a recommendable act of purification, etc.; when there is a need to use such types of water, then they are not disliked. Likewise, when there is a need for using disliked vessels or clothes, they are no longer disliked. And it is disliked to enter a restroom with anything which contains the remembrance of Allah, without need; it is disliked to look around during the prayer, or to spread out the arms during prostration or make slight movements, etc. except for a need.

BENEFIT: A need (and not a necessity) can be a cause for a prohibition to be legalised when its prohibition is light, such as those things whose prohibition is due to what it leads to, rather than being prohibited in and of itself. For example: the lawfulness of wearing silk due to a medical problem such as itching and inflammation; [likewise,] the lawfulness of buying date-palm trees (*al-'Arāyā*) for ripe dates by estimation due to a necessity; [likewise,] the lawfulness of postponing a commercial exchange between two traders if one of the articles being weighed is currency. There are also other issues and scenarios.

[9] Recorded by Al-Bukhari (39) but not by Muslim as pointed out by Ibn Hajr al-'Asqalānī in *Fath al-Bārī* (1/94).

والثالثة: الضرورة تقدر بقدرها

3. A NECESSITY IS MEASURED BY ITS EXTENT

That is, when a prohibition is legalised due to a necessity, it is not absolutely legitimate, but rather it is bound by the extent of its necessity; if the necessity ends, abstaining (from the prohibited matter) is obligatory because it was legalised due to its necessity and once it is no longer necessary, it returns to its (original) state (of prohibition). This applies to carrion being legalised due to a necessity; it may be eaten according to the amount it takes to stay alive. Other examples include purification by *tayammum* and the purification of one who is perpetually in a state of impurity (due to an illness or condition); they are bound by time due to them being forms of purification due to a necessity only. Likewise, compulsion in divorce initiated from the side of the husband (*al-Tallāq*) or wife (*al-Khula'*), taking an oath, freeing a slave, or selling, renting, admission, etc.; whatever these matters compel one to do are not applicable (because he was compelled); if one is compelled to do any of the above he may do so but if he does any of the above without being compelled, then it is correctly applicable, as he was not forced. For example:

- If one is compelled to utter a single pronouncement of divorce, but then he utters it more than once.

- Or one is compelled to divorce his wife Hind but he divorces his second wife Fātimah instead.
- Or one is compelled to sell his house but he sells his slave instead.
- Or one is compelled to admit the amount of a dirham but he admits a dinar instead, etc.

Allah knows best.

القاعدة الثالثة: أحكام الوسائل كأحكام المقاصد، وما لا يتم الواجب إلا به فهو واجب

MAXIM THREE: THE RULINGS ON THE MEANS ARE LIKE THE RULINGS ON THE ENDS; WHATEVER IS NECESSARY TO COMPLETE AN OBLIGATION IS ITSELF AN OBLIGATION

Meaning: the means of legislative rules, i.e. their processes and integral factors, are given the same rulings as the ends, because whatever cannot be completed except by a particular factor, then that factor falls under its ruling by necessity, as it is equally required.

Thus, if something is commanded, then whatever factor is required to complete it is also commanded. Whatever is necessary to complete an obligation, is itself an obligation; whatever is necessary to complete a recommended act is itself recommended; if something is prohibited, then every type of procedure, means and process which leads to that thing is prohibited likewise, whether it is prohibited or disliked.

Examples include the obligatory prayer, zakāt, fasting, Hajj, 'umrah and jihād. [Likewise,] individual obligations and fulfilling obligatory rights, such as the rights of Allah, one's parents, relatives, spouses, leaders, etc. Whatever is necessary to complete these aforementioned things, is itself obligatory, such as walking to the place of prayer, purifying oneself for its purpose, covering oneself (appropriately for prayer), as well as all its (other) conditions, and endeavouring to carry them out.

As for the recommended acts, then examples include the optional prayer, giving charity, fasting, a supererogatory Hajj and 'umrah, visiting the sick, attending a gathering of remembrance, etc. Whatever is necessary to complete these aforementioned things is itself recommended, such as walking to a particular place, etc.

The same applies to prohibitions, such as *shirk* (associating partners with Allah in worship), murder, fornication, consuming alcohol, taking interest, etc. All processes, which lead to these aforementioned matters, are prohibited and forbidden; This [also] applies to every trick that is used to obtain interest and any other prohibited matter, as one is to observe the intention behind it and its eventual result, such as the matter of *'īna*[10], the prohibition of taking *ribā al-fadl*[11], *nikah al-muhallil*[12], etc. In the same way, the means to disliked matters are themselves disliked. Allah knows best.

---

[10] i.e. selling goods for a deferred price, then later buying them at a lesser price; it is counted as a means of taking interest and is therefore prohibited.

[11] i.e. interest by way of taking a surplus during the exchange of commodities for example.

[12] A marriage contracted with a previously-divorced woman with the intention of conducting a complete divorce in order for her to marry her previous husband again.

القاعدة الرابعة: المشقة تجلب التيسير

MAXIM FOUR: HARDSHIP ENTAILS EASE

This is because the Sharia is built on compassion, mercy and ease, due to the saying of the Most High:

﴿ وَمَا جَعَلَ عَلَيْكُمْ فِي ٱلدِّينِ مِنْ حَرَجٍ ﴾

> **"And (Allah) has not laid upon you in Religion any hardship." [22:78]**

Accordingly, actions are of two kinds: one type which the legally responsible person is unable to carry out for which Allah does not burden him over, due to His saying- the Most High:

﴿ لَا يُكَلِّفُ ٱللَّهُ نَفْسًا إِلَّا وُسْعَهَا ﴾

> **"Allah burdens not a person beyond his scope." [2:286]**

The other type covers what one is able to carry out but is not burdened with either doing it or leaving it as (Allah's) divine wisdom does not require it.

As for whatever (Allah's) divine wisdom does require, then He either commands or prohibits (depending on what it is). If a matter would lead to hardship and difficulty, then inevitably it entails lightening and easing, either by omitting it entirely or partly.

This principle applies to various categories of fiqh, including acts of worship like:

- The permission to perform *tayammum* when a difficulty would arise in using water (to purify oneself), as detailed in the books of *fiqh*;
- Sitting in prayer when standing would cause difficulty, in both the obligatory and optional prayers;
- Shortening the prayer during a journey and combining between two prayers; etc.

Examples of acts of worship which may be lightened:

- Pardoning the attendance of *jum'ah* (Friday prayer) or the congregational prayer (*jamā'ah*);
- Advancing the payment of zakāt;
- And other acts of worship, transactions, marital issues and felonies.

And examples of actions being lightened unrestrictedly include communal acts which are either obligatory or *sunnah*, and acting on assumption when there is difficulty in ascertaining something with certainty.

القاعدة الخامسة: درء المفاسد أولى من جلب المصالح، وإن تزاحم مصلحتان قدم أرجحهما، وقد يعرض للمفضول ما يصيره أفضل من غيره، وإن تزاحم مفسدتان فعل أهونهما

MAXIM FIVE: REPELLING HARM TAKES PRECEDENCE OVER OBTAINING BENEFIT; IF TWO BENEFITS CLASH, THEN THE PREDOMINANT ONE TAKES PRECEDENCE, AND THE PREFERRED ONE IS EXAMINED FOR WHAT MAKES IT BETTER THAN OTHERS; AND IF TWO HARMS CLASH, THE LESSER OF THE TWO IS CARRIED OUT.

This principle is of tremendous benefit and its subdivisions are expansive; it comprises four rules:

[1] REPELLING HARM TAKES PRECEDENCE OVER OBTAINING BENEFIT

Know, that harms (*mafāsid*) are prohibitions and disliked things, just as benefits (*masālih*) are obligations and recommended things. If a matter revolves between obtaining a benefit and repelling a harm, then (repelling a harm) takes precedence. In fact, the prescribed course of action is repelling the harm even if it means the benefit is missed. This is because the benefit is neither completed nor perfected except by abandoning the harm, as such, abstaining from vices takes precedence over being distinguished by virtues.

Accordingly, prayer in an unlawfully acquired land is not correct, as with the case of stolen garments; or in the case of a pilgrim, such as a man wearing silk; (and) performing ablution with stolen water, even though ablution and prayer are acts of worship, due to them consisting of a prohibited act, which therefore renders them incorrect.

[2] IF TWO CLEAR BENEFITS CLASH, AND IT IS NOT POSSIBLE TO DO THEM BOTH, AND IN THE EVENT OF DOING ONE THE OTHER WILL BE MISSED, THE PREDOMINANT OF THE TWO TAKES PRECEDENCE

If one of the [benefits] is recommended while the other is obligatory, then the obligatory one takes precedence. Due to this, absolute optional acts performed by someone who is in danger of losing (more pressing) duties is incorrect; if (an obligatory) prayer is announced (by *iqāmah*) and time is short, optional prayer is not correct. Likewise, whoever is required to make up (the fasts of) Ramadān, it is not correct for him to fast (optional fasts) until he makes up what is required of him. Similarly, whoever is required to perform the (obligatory) Hajj, it is not correct for him to perform an optional one, or Hajj on someone else's behalf.

If both [benefits] are obligatory, then the one that is more of an obligation and confirmed takes precedence. As such, an obligation which is one of the foundations of the Sharia (for example) takes precedence over the obligation of carrying out a vow; the right of Allah the Most High is an obligation which takes precedence over obedience to whoever it is obligatory to obey (other than Him) such as the parent, the husband, the leader, etc.; the right of the husband takes precedence over the right of the parents; the individual obligation takes precedence over the communal obligation; if both [benefits] are recommended, the better of the two takes precedence. As such, the regular Sunnah prayers take precedence over the other optional prayers; acts of worship that contain exceeding benefit take precedence over those whose benefit is inferior.

[3] A PREFERRED MATTER IS EXAMINED FOR WHAT MAKES IT BETTER THAN OTHERS; AND THAT IS EVIDENT BY ANY GIVEN CAUSE CONNECTED TO THE PREFERRED ACTION; IT IS THEN NECESSARY TO PREFER IT OVER THE OTHERS

Some of the causes of preference (*asbāb al-tafdīl*):

- The preferred action is instructed specifically in that location or time such as the remembrances and supplications (*adhkār*) in the prayer and after it; appointed remembrances in their specific times and due to specific reasons are better than reciting the Quran during such times, keeping in mind that reciting the Quran is in and of itself more virtuous than supplication. Yet, when supplication is coupled with particularisation (*takhsīs*), it is better (than reciting Quran).
- The preferred action consists of a benefit that is not found in the matter being preferred over, such as reconciliation; an exceeding benefit that is not possible to obtain by the matter being preferred over; or the preferred matter includes the repelling of a harm that it is suspected will occur if the thing being preferred over is carried out.
- The preferred action would increase the benefit to one's heart more than the matter being preferred over; as Imam Ahmad ﷺ said to someone who asked him about some actions: "See what is better for your heart, and do that."

The causes of preference are a great many; what I have mentioned is sufficient for one to be mindful of the others.

[4] IF TWO HARMS CLASH, THE LESSER OF THE TWO IS CARRIED OUT

Meaning: the lighter of the two. As such, if something disliked and something forbidden clash in such a way that one of them has to be carried out, the disliked matter is done in order to repel the forbidden matter by committing the lesser of the two evils; for example, acquiring money from a doubtful place instead of money which is forbidden, if it is necessary to take one of the two.

If two forbidden acts clash, then the lesser of the two is carried out. As such, wearing a silk garment takes precedence over a stolen garment, or in the case of extreme hunger, meat from a dead animal which is normally lawful when sacrificed, such as the meat of a dead sheep, etc. takes precedence over the meat of a dead animal which is not lawful when sacrificed, such as a dog, etc.

If two disliked matters clash, the lighter of the two is done. As such, wealth, which is forbidden in a slight manner, is lighter than wealth that is forbidden in a great manner. The strength and weakness of a disliked matter is according to the insignificance or greatness of the unlawful matter.

القاعدة السادسة: النية والإسلام والعقل والتمييز شرط لصحة جميع الأعمال إلا التمييز في الحج والعمرة، والردة تبطل سائر الأعمال

MAXIM SIX: INTENTION, ISLAM, SANITY AND TAMYĪZ ARE STIPULATIONS FOR THE CORRECTNESS OF ALL ACTIONS, EXCEPT TAMYĪZ DURING HAJJ AND 'UMRAH; APOSTACY NULLIFIES ALL ACTIONS.

As such, all acts of worship, be they obligatory or supererogatory, are not correct except when a Muslim who is sane and *mumayyiz*[13] intends to carry them out, for these are the conditions of correctness which apply to all actions.

Acts of worship without intention, or without the intention of the doer, are invalid and not considered. Likewise, all the actions of the disbeliever (are invalid) until he embraces Islam; if he embraces Islam, he is not required to make these actions up. The insane person's acts of worship are not correct, and neither are they obligated on him due to the absence of his sanity and intention. The child (*tifal*), i.e. who is below the age of seven

[13] The age of *tamyīz*, which some scholars specify as seven years, refers to the age in which a child is able to distinguish between right and wrong; the *mumayyiz* is anyone who has reached the age of *tamyīz* and over.

according to what is widely accepted, or, according to the correct opinion, the child who understands speech and is able to respond to a question correctly (i.e. he has reached the age of *tamyīz*): his acts of worship are incorrect due to the absence of his intention, or because he is not expected to be able to do so, except in the case of Hajj and 'umrah, for they are both correct, even if the child's guardian places the ihrām on him from his own wealth, i.e. the guardian intends (the Hajj or 'umrah) on the child's behalf and carries out whatever rites the child is unable to do.

Therefore, Hajj and 'umrah differ from the rest of the actions in several aspects, including:

- *Tamyīz* is not a condition for their correctness as you now know, but it is stipulated for the correctness of all other actions.
- Whoever begins the act of an optional prayer, fast, etc. then it is not binding on him to complete it except in the case of Hajj and 'umrah.
- Whoever is obliged to perform the (obligatory) Islamic Hajj, but wears the ihrām to carry out an optional Hajj, or to perform it on behalf of someone else, or for the purpose of fulfilling a vow, it is not correct and his intention is changed, without his choice, to carry out the (obligatory) Islamic Hajj.
- Every action which, if it is nullified (by a matter) and one exits from it, it is not obligatory on the doer to complete it except in the case of Hajj and 'umrah. Therefore, if (the state of ihrām) was nullified by participating in sexual intercourse (for example), completing (the Hajj or 'umrah) and repeating it is obligatory.

BENEFIT: *Taklīf* (the state of responsibility), which refers to sanity and reaching the age of maturity (*bulūgh*), is a condition for the obligation of all actions. As such, no actions are obligated on the young person, the child who is below the age of maturity and the person who is insane; once a child reaches 10 complete years, he is scolded when he leaves the prayer, fasting, and their like as a matter of disciplining and training only.

As for apostasy from Islam: it is to say or do something during an action which would remove one from Islam, as is detailed in the chapter on the ruling of the apostate (in the books of *fiqh*); it nullifies every action carried out, inlcuding ablution, bathing, tayammum, the entire prayer, fasting, Hajj, 'umrah, etc. due to the saying of Allah the Most High:

﴿ لَئِنْ أَشْرَكْتَ لَيَحْبَطَنَّ عَمَلُكَ وَلَتَكُونَنَّ مِنَ ٱلْخَٰسِرِينَ ﴾

> **"If you join others in worship with Allah, (then) surely (all) your deeds will be in vain..."** [39: 65]

As for the actions one did during his state of Islam and before his apostasy, is it also nullified by the apostasy even if he returns to Islam? The correct view is that the actions one did before apostasy return to him if he embraces Islam based on the statement of Allah the Most High:

﴿ وَمَن يَرْتَدِدْ مِنكُمْ عَن دِينِهِۦ فَيَمُتْ وَهُوَ كَافِرٌ فَأُو۟لَٰٓئِكَ حَبِطَتْ أَعْمَٰلُهُمْ ﴾

"Whosoever of you turns back from his Religion and dies as a disbeliever, then his deeds will be lost..." [2: 217]

القاعدة السابعة: مخالفة الكفار مشروعة

MAXIM SEVEN: DIFFERING WITH THE DISBELIEVERS IS LEGISLATED IN THE SHARIA

This is a tremendous maxim, one that the Legislator has intended for many affairs. *Shaykh al-Islam* Ibn Taymiyyah has written a book on this subject entitled *'Iqtidā' Sirāt al-Mustaqīm fī Mukhālafat Ashab al-Jahīm*, which is both sufficient and adequate, may Allah have mercy on his soul and be pleased with him!

An example of an act which falls under this maxim is the prohibition of resembling the disbelievers in clothing and appearance, as is detailed in the chapter of rulings related to dhimmis.

Likewise, the Prophet ﷺ differed from the manner of the polytheists in many of the rites of Hajj, such as departing from 'Arafah after Maghrib and Muzdalifah before sunrise; and this is due to the statement of the Prophet ﷺ:

« من تشبه بقوم فهو منهم »

"Whoever resembles a people is from them."[14]

[14] Recorded by Abu Dawud (4031).

The precept to this maxim is: every matter which is particular to the polytheists - be they People of the Book (Jews and Christians) or others - then it is prohibited to resemble them in it. This is because resembling them outwardly leads to agreement inwardly. Moreover, it is legislated to differ with the innovators; just as it is disliked to prostate the forehead on a particular place in order to differ with the Rafidites; likewise, it is disliked to specify 'Ali ﷺ and the *Ahl al-Bayt* (the household of the Prophet) with prayers (*al-salāt*); one is to abstain from these matters in order to differ from [the Rafidites]. Allah knows best.

القاعدة الثامنة: الذكر كالأنثيين في مسائل

MAXIM EIGHT: THE MALE IS EQUAL TO TWO FEMALES IN VARIOUS MATTERS

For example:

- Inheritance;
- Blood money;
- The *'Aqīqah* (the ritual sacrifice of an animal on the occasion of a child's birth) for a girl is one sheep and two for a boy;
- Giving testimony;
- Freeing from slavery;
- Gifting (wealth) to children during one's lifetime (as oppose to leaving them to divide it after one's death);
- Etc.

And Allah knows best.

القاعدة التاسعة: إذا اجتمعت عبادتان من جنس واحد واستوت أفعالهما اكتفي منهما بفعل واحد

MAXIM NINE: IF TWO ACTS OF WORSHIP FROM THE SAME TYPE COME TOGETHER AND CARRYING THEM BOTH OUT IS THE SAME, THEN IT IS SUFFICIENT TO DO ONE OF THEM

This occurs in two ways:

[1] One is able to achieve two acts of worship by carrying out one action. In this case, it is stipulated that one intends both actions together, according to what is popularly held by the scholars. Examples of this include:

- Whoever is in a state of major and minor impurity, then the (Hanbalī) ***madhhab*** affirms that it is sufficient for him to carry out the major purification (i.e. the *ghusl* [ritual bath]) to cleanse himself from both types (of impurity).
- For the pilgrim who intends to combine Hajj and 'umrah (i.e. the *qirān* form of Hajj), according to the popularly held position (in the *madhhab*), it is sufficient for him to carry out one set of *tawāf* and *sa'ī*.

[2] One is able to achieve one of the two acts of worship by intention, and the other act is waived thereby. Examples of this include:

- When entering a masjid and the call to commence the prayer in congregation is announced (*iqāmah*), then the prayer of entering the masjid (*al-tahiyyah*) is waived when one joins the congregational prayer.
- When a pilgrim intending 'umrah arrives in Mecca, he may begin with the *tawāf* of 'umrah and the *tawāf* of arrival (*al-qudūm*) is waived from him.
- If a Muslim finds the imām in *rukū'* (the bowing position), and he utters the commencement of the prayer which is signalled by saying "*Allāhu Akbar*" (*takbīrah al-ihrām*), then uttering "*Allāhu Akbar*" before making *rukū'* is waived. This is according to the popularly held opinion of the scholars.
- If *'Eid* and Friday (*Jumu'ah*) are on the same day, then it is sufficient to attend one of the two prayers.
- If the time of sacrifice (on *'Eid al-Adhā*) and the ritual sacrifice of an animal on the occasion of a child's birth (*al-'aqīqah*) coincide, then the *'aqīqah* takes the place of the *adhiyah* (*'Eid* sacrifice).
- Likewise, if the reasons which obligate one to offer expiation come together, and overlap in matters of making an oath, Hajj, fasting, *zihār*[15], etc., then if one

[15] *Al-Zihār* (الظهار): when a husband prohibits himself from enjoying marital relations with his wife by insulting her with the following saying, "You are like my mother's back!" This is said in order to liken her to a relative he is prohibited to marry. *Al-Zihār* is prohibited and has implications in divorce

carries out the expiation for one reason, it takes place and absolves him from the other expiations due.

---

cases. In reference to the expiation, Allah states in Sūrah al-Mujādilah, verses 2 to 4:

﴿ ٱلَّذِينَ يُظَٰهِرُونَ مِنكُم مِّن نِّسَآئِهِم مَّا هُنَّ أُمَّهَٰتِهِمْ ۖ إِنْ أُمَّهَٰتُهُمْ إِلَّا ٱلَّٰٓـِٔى وَلَدْنَهُمْ ۚ وَإِنَّهُمْ لَيَقُولُونَ مُنكَرًا مِّنَ ٱلْقَوْلِ وَزُورًا ۚ وَإِنَّ ٱللَّهَ لَعَفُوٌّ غَفُورٌ • وَٱلَّذِينَ يُظَٰهِرُونَ مِن نِّسَآئِهِمْ ثُمَّ يَعُودُونَ لِمَا قَالُوا۟ فَتَحْرِيرُ رَقَبَةٍ مِّن قَبْلِ أَن يَتَمَآسَّا ۚ ذَٰلِكُمْ تُوعَظُونَ بِهِۦ ۚ وَٱللَّهُ بِمَا تَعْمَلُونَ خَبِيرٌ • فَمَن لَّمْ يَجِدْ فَصِيَامُ شَهْرَيْنِ مُتَتَابِعَيْنِ مِن قَبْلِ أَن يَتَمَآسَّا ۖ فَمَن لَّمْ يَسْتَطِعْ فَإِطْعَامُ سِتِّينَ مِسْكِينًا ۚ ذَٰلِكَ لِتُؤْمِنُوا۟ بِٱللَّهِ وَرَسُولِهِۦ ۚ وَتِلْكَ حُدُودُ ٱللَّهِ ۗ وَلِلْكَٰفِرِينَ عَذَابٌ أَلِيمٌ ﴾

"Those who pronounce *al-zihār* among you [to separate] from their wives - they are not [consequently] their mothers. Their mothers are none but those who gave birth to them. And indeed, they are saying an objectionable statement and a falsehood. But indeed, Allah is Pardoning and Forgiving. And those who pronounce *al-zihār* from their wives and then [wish to] go back on what they said - then [there must be] the freeing of a slave before they touch one another. That is what you are admonished thereby; and Allah is Acquainted with what you do. And he who does not find [a slave] - then a fast for two months consecutively before they touch one another; and he who is unable - then the feeding of sixty poor persons. That is for you to believe [completely] in Allah and His Messenger; and those are the limits [set by] Allah. And for the disbelievers is a painful punishment."

القاعدة العاشرة: العبرة بالغالب ولاعبرة بالنادر

MAXIM TEN: CONSIDERATION IS GIVEN TO THE GENERAL RULE AND NOT THE EXCEPTIONAL CIRCUMSTANCE

This means that issues that agree in routine and reason, but differ in some circumstances whereby a legislated reason cannot be found for it, then in such cases, the general ruling is adhered to even if there is no (legislated) reason. Travelling demonstrates this: many permits are legislated with respect to travelling because it is considered a kind of hardship, such as shortening and combining prayers, breaking a fast, etc. As such, if a traveller does not find any difficulty in travelling at all, it is not said to him that he is not allowed any of the permits of travelling due to the absence of the rightful reason (for such permits). Rather, all of the permits of travelling are permissible for him to take, in conjunction with exceptional circumstances being considered by general rulings.

Likewise, a resident combining two congregational prayers due to it raining; this is permissible for whoever is in the masjid, home and whose way to the masjid is a roofed passage.

The same applies to forbidden matters which are forbidden due to their harm; suppose a person is found who is not harmed by them, they are still forbidden to him just as they are to others[16].

[16] This is because consideration is given to general rule and not the exceptional circumstance; an example to illustrate this is the matter of intoxicants which are forbidden due to their harm; if a person was unaffected by intoxicants, they would still be forbidden to him and others because his case is an exception and consideration is not given to it.

القاعدة الحادية عشرة: اليقين لا يزول بالشك

MAXIM ELEVEN: CERTAINTY IS NOT REMOVED BY DOUBT

I.e. when a person verifies a matter, then falls into doubt during it, is the matter no longer verified? The basic rule is the verified matter remains as it is and therefore the matter remains as the verification first indicated.

What if a person doubts he married a woman? In this case they may not take part in sexual intercourse due to the ruling of prohibition. On the other hand, if he doubts whether he divorced his wife or not, then it means he has not, and they may take part in sexual intercourse due to (their) marriage.

Likewise, if one doubts the validity of his *wuḍū'* (i.e. whether it has been broken or not) after he was certain he was in a state of purity, or vice versa, or he doubts the number of prayer units, number of circumambulations around the Ka'ba, *sa'ī*, throwing of pebbles at the *jamarāt,* etc. then he carries on based on his (previous) certainty and it is the minimum[17].

[17] As such, if he was certain he was in a state of purity, then doubted whether he invalidated it, he carries on based on his certainty. If he doubts the number of prayer units he has performed, then he should go by the minimum number that he is certain of praying and complete the number of units he doubted.

However, the basic rule can be vague with respect to returning to it when doubt appears; as such there is a need to mention several principles related to specific rulings:

The Basic Rule Regarding Things is Purity

If a person's body or clothing is touched by water or moisture, or he steps on dung, or dung or bones fall into water, and he doubts its purity or its impurity, then he should consider it pure in following the basic rule, even if he thinks it is more likely to be impure; this is because it is pure until he can verify its impurity.

The Basic Rule Regarding Foods is that they are Lawful

This is because Allah the Most High created for His creation all that is on the earth in order to benefit from by eating, drinking, etc.; and He permitted this to them. As such, no foods or drinks are prohibited except what Allah and His Messenger ﷺ prohibit.

The Basic Rule Regarding Sexual Intercourse is Prohibition

Sexual intercourse is not permitted except in the cases Allah and His Messenger ﷺ have permitted, i.e. marriage or (slave) ownership, which is based on the saying of the Most High:

﴿وَٱلَّذِينَ هُمۡ لِفُرُوجِهِمۡ حَٰفِظُونَ • إِلَّا عَلَىٰٓ أَزۡوَٰجِهِمۡ أَوۡ مَا مَلَكَتۡ
أَيۡمَٰنُهُمۡ فَإِنَّهُمۡ غَيۡرُ مَلُومِينَ • فَمَنِ ٱبۡتَغَىٰ وَرَآءَ ذَٰلِكَ فَأُوْلَٰٓئِكَ هُمُ
ٱلۡعَادُونَ﴾

> "And those who guard their private parts; except from their wives or those their right hands possess, for indeed, they are not to be blamed; but whoever seeks beyond that, then they are the transgressors." [70:29-31]

If doubt occurs in any given circumstance, is sexual intercourse permitted or not? The basic rule is prohibition until we verify its lawfulness.

The Basic Rule Regarding the Life of the Protected Citizen, his Wealth and Honour, is Prohibition

As such, these things are not lawful except when they are taken by right; i.e. the basic rule regarding the protected citizen – and he is either a Muslim, a *dhimmī* disbeliever or one who has a covenant of security – is that his wealth, life and honour is sacred, and it is not permissible to take any of these things in any circumstance until we verify the lawfulness to do so; and we cannot verify the lawfulness of such a matter except by a specific legal text (i.e. the Quran or Sunnah).

It is not permitted (for an Islamic government) to take the life of a Muslim except: the married person who commits adultery, in the case of a life for a life and that of one who exits the religion of Islam.

Likewise, the protected citizen who is a disbeliever: it is not permissible (for the Islamic government) to kill him or cut any of his limbs except for a reason that necessitates it in the Sharia.

The same applied to the wealth of the Muslim, the *dhimmī* and whoever has a covenant of security: none of it is lawful except for a Sharia-based right, and the same applies to their honour.

The details of the Sharia rights regarding lives, wealth and honour are a great many; it is not possible to mention them all in this short work, but the *fuqahā* have spoken of these matters in the books of *fiqh* and rulings, so refer to them.

The Basic Rule Regarding Acts of Worship is one of Prohibition

Therefore, nothing is legislated in the religion except what Allah and His Messenger ﷺ legislated.

The Basic Rule Regarding Customary Acts is one of Lawfulness

Therefore, nothing customary is prohibited except for what Allah and His Messenger ﷺ prohibited.

القاعدة الثانية عشرة: العرف والعادة يرجع إليه في كل حكم به الشارع ولم يحده بحد

MAXIM TWELVE: CUSTOM AND HABITS BOTH RETURN TO EVERY RULING THE LEGISLATOR MAKES BUT DOES NOT CONFINE

This is a broad principle that is applied in transactions, rights, etc. Every ruling requires two things:

1. Knowledge of its limit;
2. Knowledge of its definition.

After this the Sharia ruling is applied to it. If we find that the Legislator has ruled something as obligatory, recommended, prohibited, disliked or lawful, and He has confined it, explained it and distinguished it, then we return to the explanation of the Legislator, as is the case with the command to pray and the mention of its virtue and reward: the Legislator has confined it and mentioned its detailed rulings which distinguish it from other acts of worship, therefore we return to what Allah and His Messenger ﷺ have limited it to. The same applies to zakāt, fasting and Hajj: the Legislator has explained it so clearly, that no doubt remains.

As for when the Legislator rules on a matter but does not confine it, then it is applied to the slaves (of Allah) according to their custom and habit, and it is clarified to them to do so, as is the case with respect to the statement of Allah the Most High:

﴿ وَعَاشِرُوهُنَّ بِٱلْمَعْرُوفِ ﴾

"And live with them (your wives) in kindness." [4:19]

Both kindness in the Sharia and kindness according to reason are applicable in this verse. Another example is His statement:

﴿ وَأْمُرْ بِٱلْعُرْفِ ﴾

"...enjoin what is good." [7:199]

Numerous issues fall under this principle:

- Allah has ordered being good to one's parents, relatives, orphans, the poor and wayfarers, as well as being good to the entire creation. Therefore, all that is included in the word good (*ihsān*) which people practice customarily, then it applies in the commands of the Sharia, because Allah generalised it, and good is the opposite and contrast of evil, as it is devoid of any form of good, be it in speech, action or in giving wealth. The Prophet ﷺ said in an authentic hadith:

  « كل معروف صدقة »

  "Every good act is a charity."[18]

[18] Recorded by al-Bukhārī (6021).

This is a clear text that indicates that every act a slave (of Allah) does to others which is a type of good, then it is counted as an act of charity.

Likewise, Allah and His Messenger ﷺ stipulated in commutative contracts (*mu'āwadāt*) and donation contracts (*tabarri'āt*) that both parties are satisfied, but they did not stipulate a specific wording for such contracts to apply, or any actions which indicate that the contract and satisfaction of the objective has been achieved. Accordingly, scholars state: "The contract is set by whatever statement or action indicates it." However, they exempt some issues and stipulate that a statement must be made due to the potential harm (if it is not made verbally), such as marriage; the scholars state that it is necessary to accept verbally; likewise, in the case of divorce, it cannot occur except by statement or writing.

- Contracts in which taking possession is stipulated, refers to whatever people consider taking possession to be; and this differs according to the circumstance.

  Likewise, in the case of guarding, whereby people entrust the protection of wealth to a guardian. The scholars stipulate that stealing refers to taking something guarded. The definition of a guard/safe is based on custom, and therefore personal wealth can have different kinds of guardians, and other types of wealth have guardians; everything has its consideration.

- A safe-keeper who loses something or transgresses, then he is liable, for whatever people consider negligence or transgression, the ruling is connected to that.
- Whoever finds something, it is binding upon him to make it known for an entire year according to the custom, and then if he is unable to find its owner, he becomes the owner.
- Endowments in banks refer to the stipulations made by the endowers as long as they do not contradict the Sharia. If the stipulation made by the endower is unknown then the relevant habit and custom of the people is observed, then to the general custom in spending it.
- In the same light, the ruling on possession of a thing (such as a house, etc.) and its surrounding land (if applicable) is that whoever possesses something and he acts with it freely for a long period of time, then it is considered to belong to him unless a proof is presented which indicates otherwise.
- Referring back to what is customarily accepted in terms of spending on wives, relatives, possessions, employees, etc. just as Allah and His Messenger ﷺ have clarified that referral is to be made to one's customs with respect to living with wives. The term living (*ma'āshirah*) is more comprehensive than spending, and therefore includes all that occurs between the two spouses in terms of speech and action when living together and the term is entirely confined by custom.
- The menstruating woman refers to her particular habit of menstruating when she is unable to distinguish whether

she has stopped menstruating or not. If she is excused from knowing this because of forgetfulness, etc. then she should refer to the habit of the women in her family, otherwise the habit of the women of her land.

- Defects, fraud and deceit all return back to custom, so whatever the people consider a defect, an act of fraud or deceit, then the ruling is based on that.
- Likewise, referring to the equivalent amount in items which are valuables, damaged goods and warranties.
- And likewise, requesting a fair dowry for the woman who is entitled to it but the amount was not stated, or the stated amount is invalid *(fāsidah)*[19]; the amount varies according to the women, times and places.

And the likes of the aforementioned examples are treated similarly by making analogies; they are many, and can be found in the books of rulings.

[19] Such as the stated dowry being a prohibited item like alcohol, or an item which does not belong to the groom like a stolen ring.